The
Airport Airplane
COLORING BOOK

Illustrated by Richard King

Plymouth Press
Plymouth, Michigan

© 1995 Plymouth Press

ISBN 1-882663-04-7 with crayons
ISBN 1-882663-05-5 without crayons

2 3 4 5 6 7 8 9 0

Printed in the United States of America

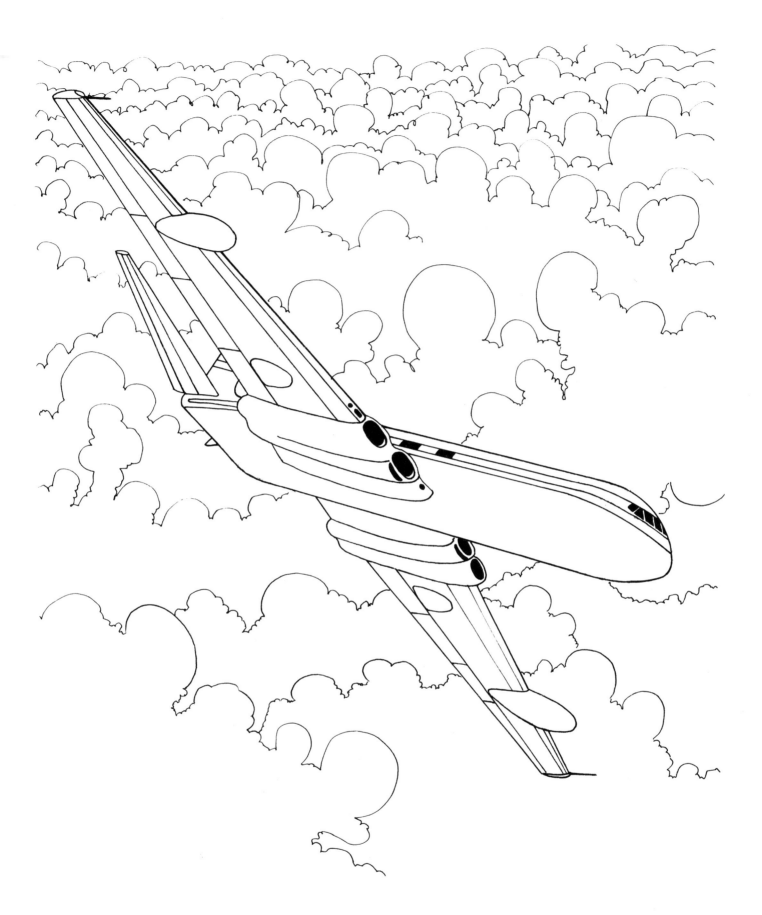

1. The world's first jetliner, the de Havilland Comet, opened a new era in transportation when it was introduced into service by British Overseas Airways Corporation (BOAC) in 1952. A prototype made its first flight in 1949.

2. The distinctive hump at the front of the fuselage—which houses the pilot's cabin and first class passenger compartment—makes the Boeing 747 easy to spot in the air or on the ground.

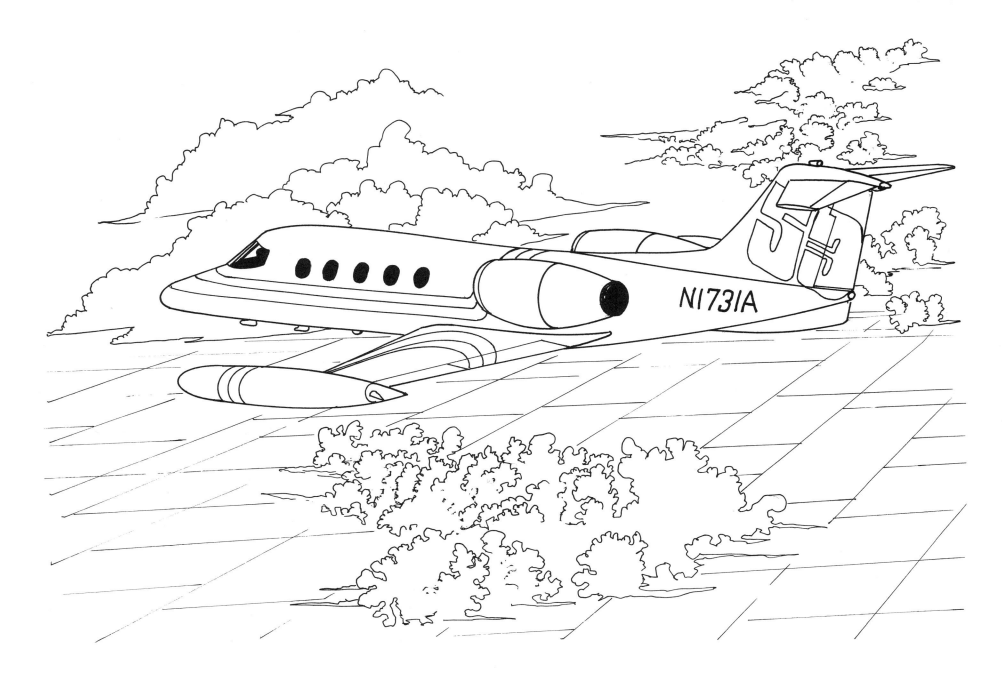

3. A standard business jet accommodating up to eight passengers, successive Learjet models have been in service since 1963.

4. The Concorde is the world's only supersonic jetliner. Built in partnership by British Aerospace and Aérospatiale, only 14 are currently in operation, seven each with British Airways and Air France.

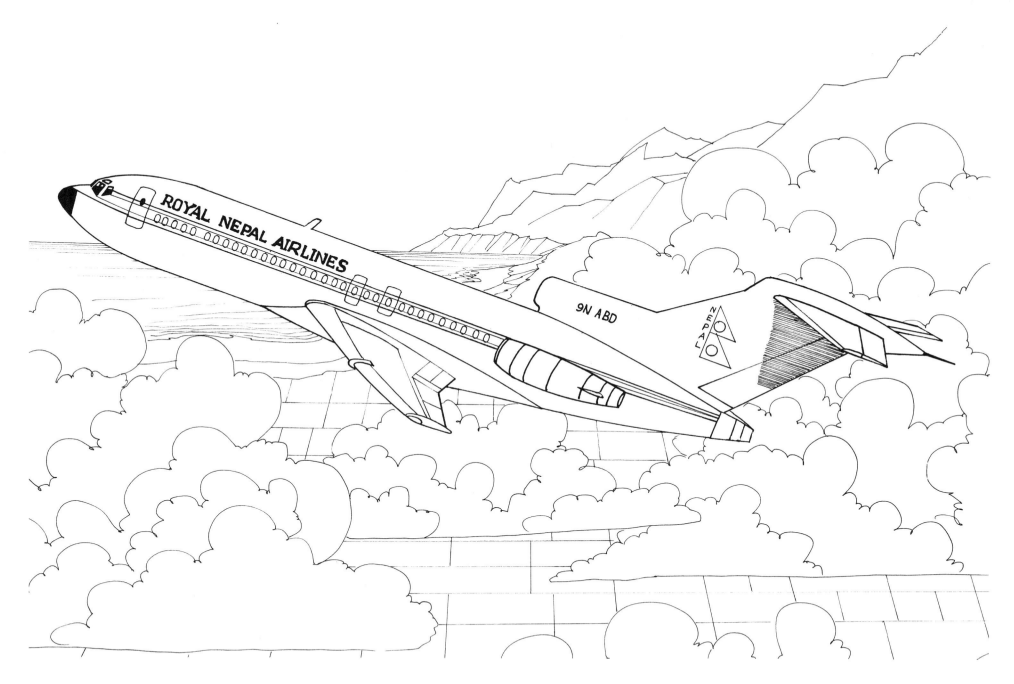

5. This Boeing 727 is operated by Royal Nepal Airlines, which began scheduled flights in 1958. The airline is based at Katmandu, Nepal, about 100 miles from Mt. Everest.

6. This Lockheed L-1011 TriStar is one of six flown by Air Canada from its hub at Mirabel International Airport in Montreal, Quebec.

7. A jumbo tri-jet, the McDonnell Douglas DC-10 has a capacity of up to 380 passengers and a range of over 4000 miles. American Airlines, based at Dallas/Ft. Worth International Airport, flies 48 DC-10s.

8. The Breguet 941 made its first flight in 1961. Designed for STOL (short take-off and landing) operation, it has an unpressurized cabin and is intended for both cargo and passenger transport.

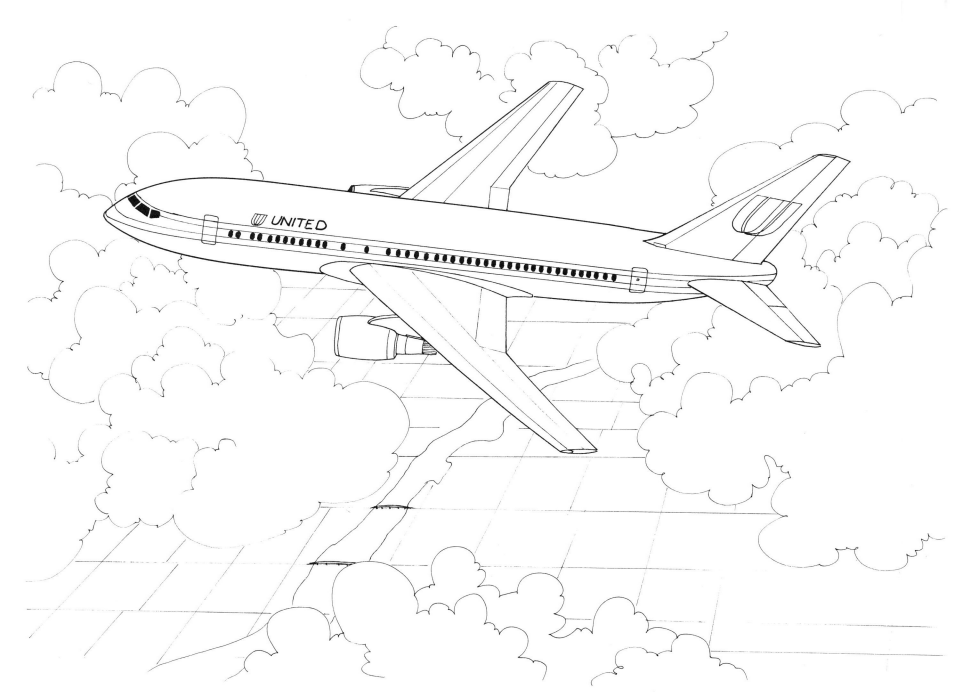

9. A wide-bodied jetliner with a capacity of up to 255 passengers, the Boeing 767 made its first flight in 1981. United Airlines, based at Chicago's O'Hare Airport, operates a fleet of 45 767s.

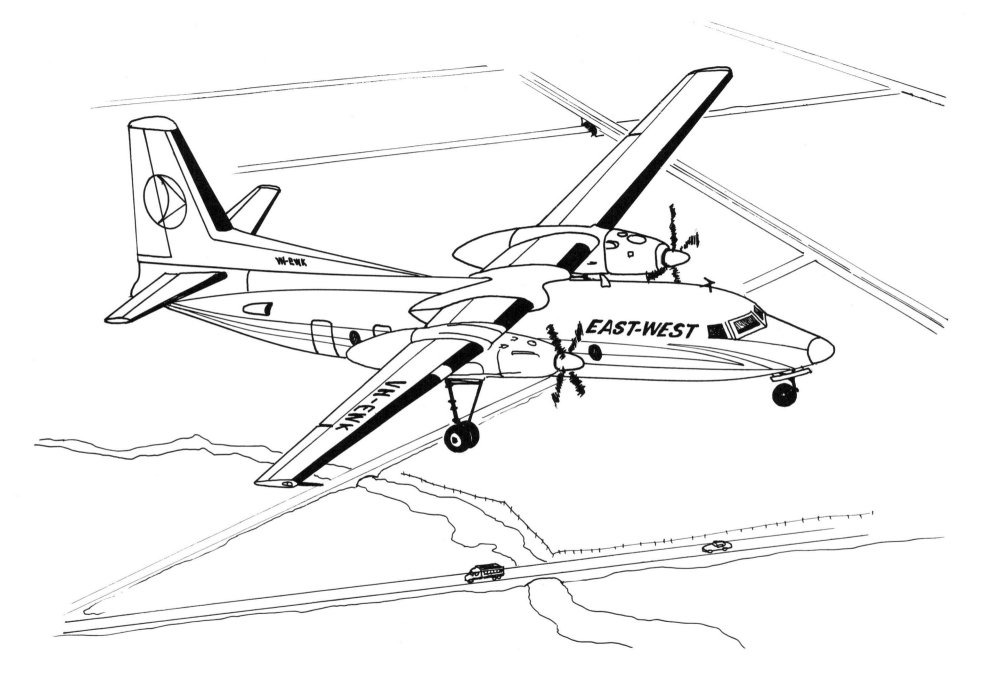

10. Designed as a short-range commuter airliner, the Fokker F.27 Friendship is a common sight at both large and small airports. In all, 786 Friendships were built at Fokker's plant near Amsterdam in the Netherlands.

11. The BAe 125 was designed as a business jet, but has performed in many roles for armed forces, including communications, troop transport, training, and air ambulance.

12. The world's first all-metal airliner, the Boeing 247 made its maiden flight in 1933. Many consider it the first modern airliner.

13. With its first flight in 1935 the Douglas DC-3 brought the convenience and speed of flight to large numbers of Americans. In all, 10,654 military and commercial models were built, many of which are still in use.

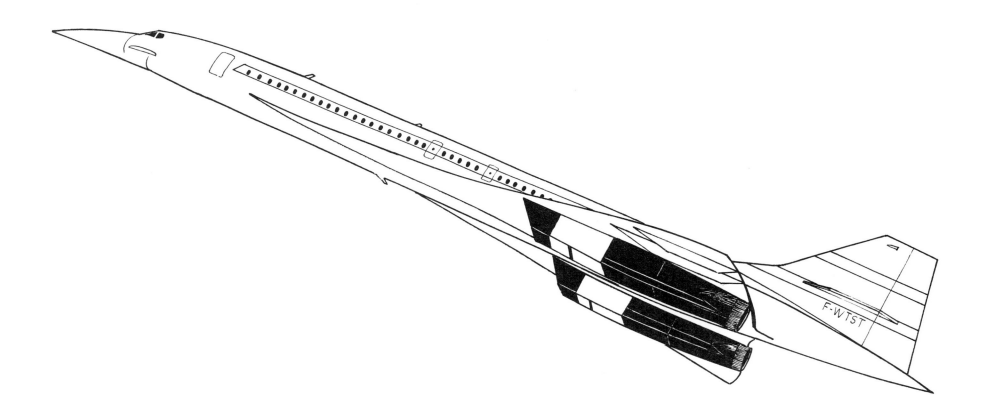

14. Soaring at 1400 miles an hour—more than twice the speed of sound—the British Aerospace/
Aérospatiale Concorde can fly 100 passengers over the Atlantic in about three hours.

15. Lockheed's Constellation, with arguably the most graceful lines of any propliner, was a frequent visitor at busy airports in the 1940s, '50s, and '60s. Advanced models could carry 95 passengers up to 3000 miles.

16. Air Canada, operating from Montreal, Canada, flies six Boeing 747s. The Boeing 747-400 model has a range of over 9000 miles.

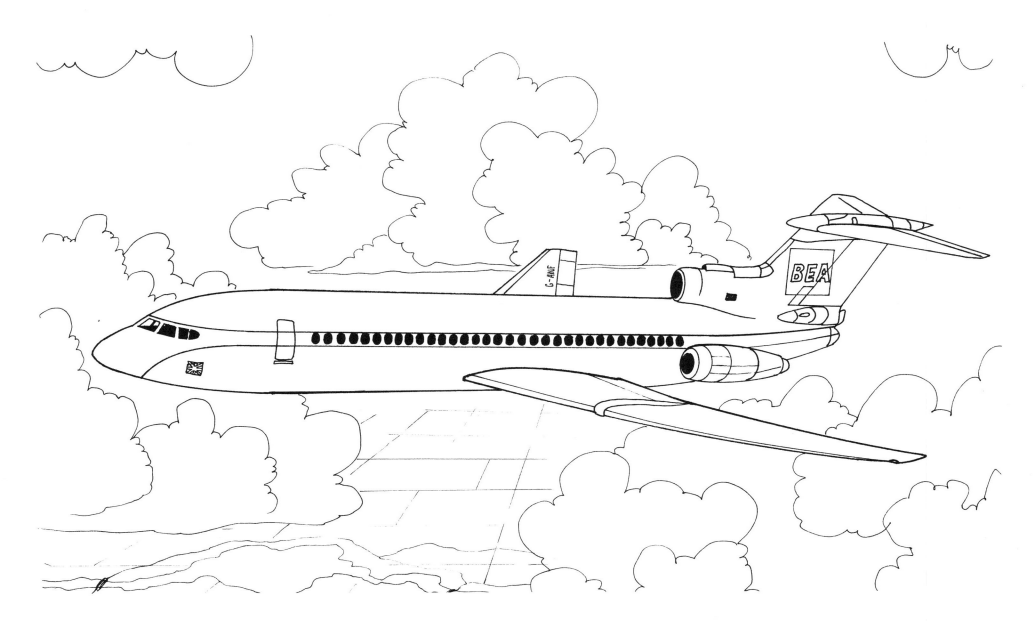

17. This early model BAe Trident was flown by British European Airways. The original Trident could carry up to 103 passengers as far as 2000 miles.

18. At more than 3000 and still counting, Boeing's 737 has been built in larger numbers than any other jetliner. Lufthansa, based in Frankfurt, Germany, operates 99 737 models.

19. The British de Havilland Comet provided the world's first passenger jetliner service on May 2, 1952, connecting London and Johannesburg via Rome, Beirut, and Khartoum.

20. The 20-seat de Havilland Canada DHC-6 Twin Otter is a versatile cargo and passenger transport. In all, 844 have been built and are in operation with more than 300 operators in over 90 countries around the globe.

21. The BAe 125 is a business aircraft which has been adapted to numerous roles, including air ambulance, troop carrying, and military trainer. With a range of 2680 miles, it can land on unpaved runways.

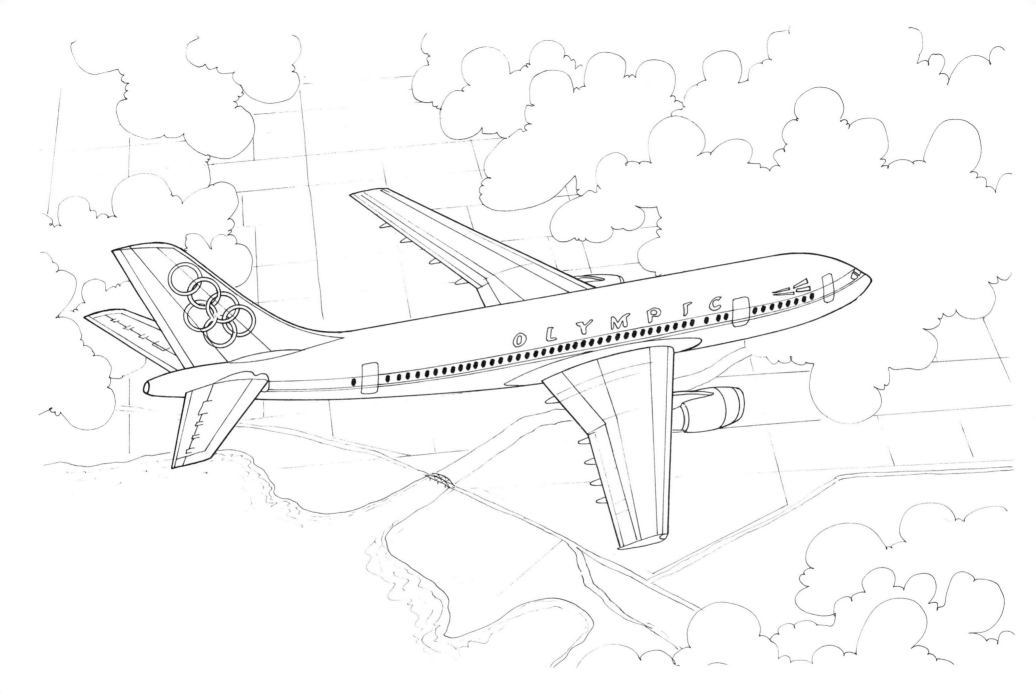

22. The Airbus A300, with a capacity of up to 345 passengers, was the first project of Airbus Industrie, a partnership of European aircraft manufacturers from five different nations. It made its first flight in 1972.

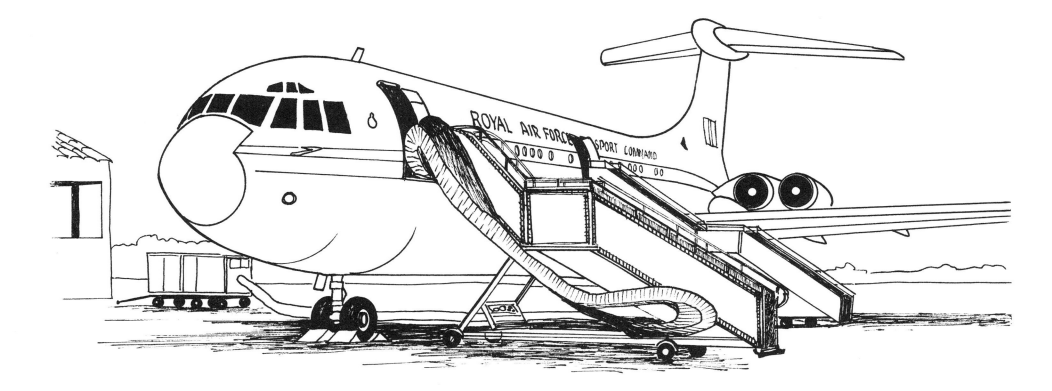

23. The Vickers VC10 is no longer in service with airlines but is still used by the United Kingdom's Royal Air Force, as pictured here.

24. The colorful paint scheme for this Douglas DC-8 was the work of a famous American abstract artist, Alexander Calder (1898-1976), who received the commision from Braniff.

25. With a capacity of 55 passengers, the BAC One-Eleven was designed for flights of up to 2000 miles. It made its first flight in 1963.

26. The Lockheed L-1011 TriStar is very similar in appearance to the McDonnell Douglas DC-10, which was built in much larger numbers. They can be told apart from the differing positions of their tail engines' exhausts.

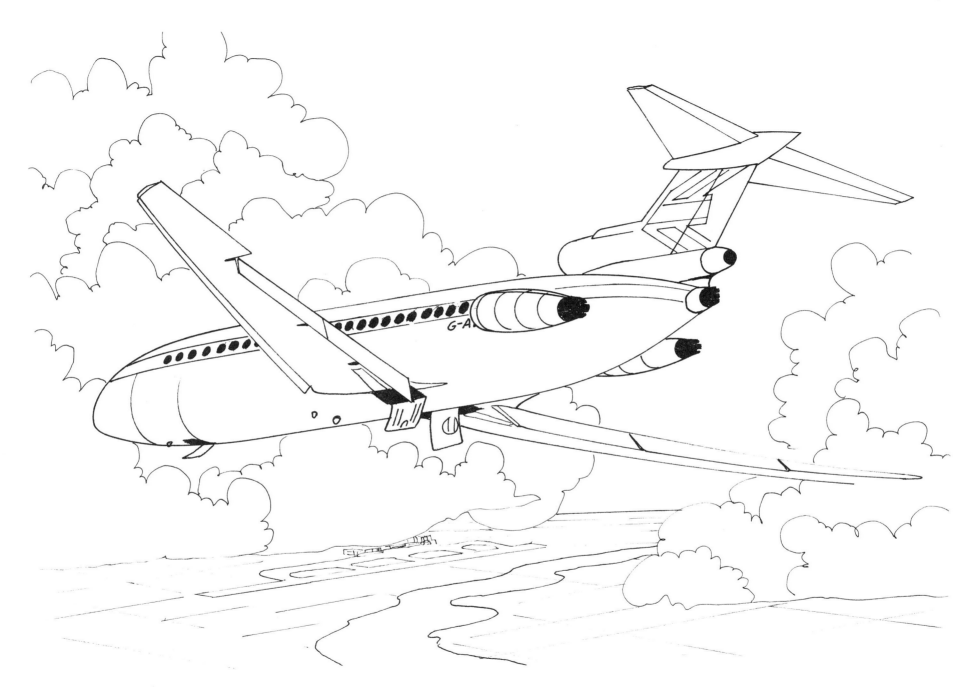

27. The BAe Trident 3 had a fuselage which was 15 feet longer than the original Trident. This allowed an increase in capacity from 103 to 180 passengers.

28. First flown in 1965, the Boeing 737 is in service with airlines all around the globe. Its many different models carry 115 to 170 passengers up to 3400 miles.

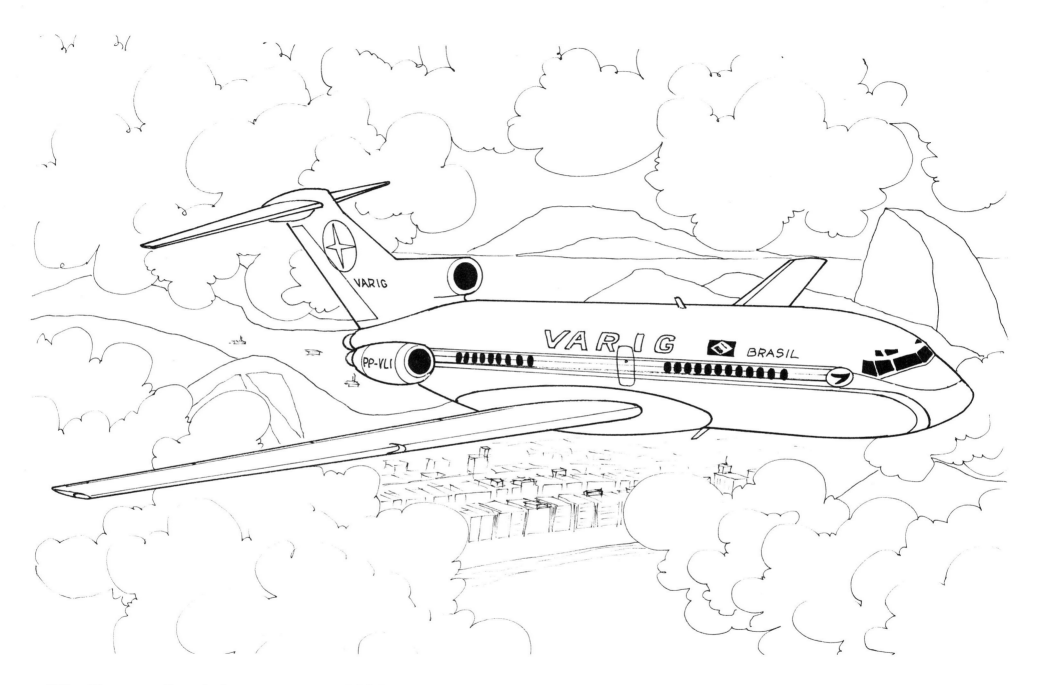

29. Flying in South America since 1928, Varig Brazilian Airlines now operates worldwide from its base in Rio de Janeiro. This Boeing 727 is one of ten flown by the airline.

30. With a range of 1800 miles and a maximum capacity of 13 passengers, over 250 Dornier Do 28 Skyservant models have been built. More than 100 were bought by the German Air Force and Navy.

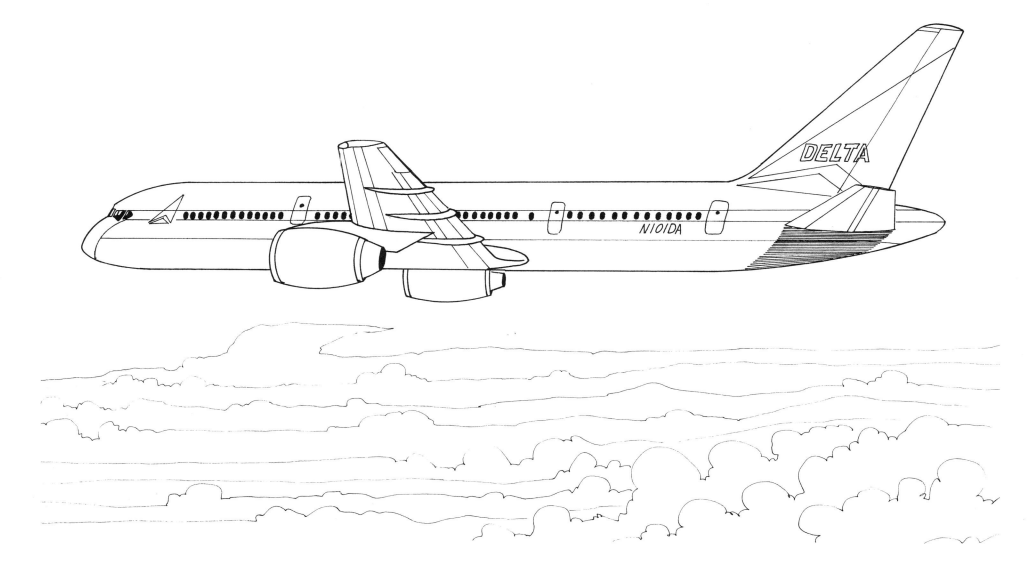

31. A modern narrow-bodied jetliner with a capacity of up to 239 passengers, the Boeing 757 can be spotted at most major airports. Delta Air Lines, based at Atlanta, Georgia, has a fleet of 59 757s.

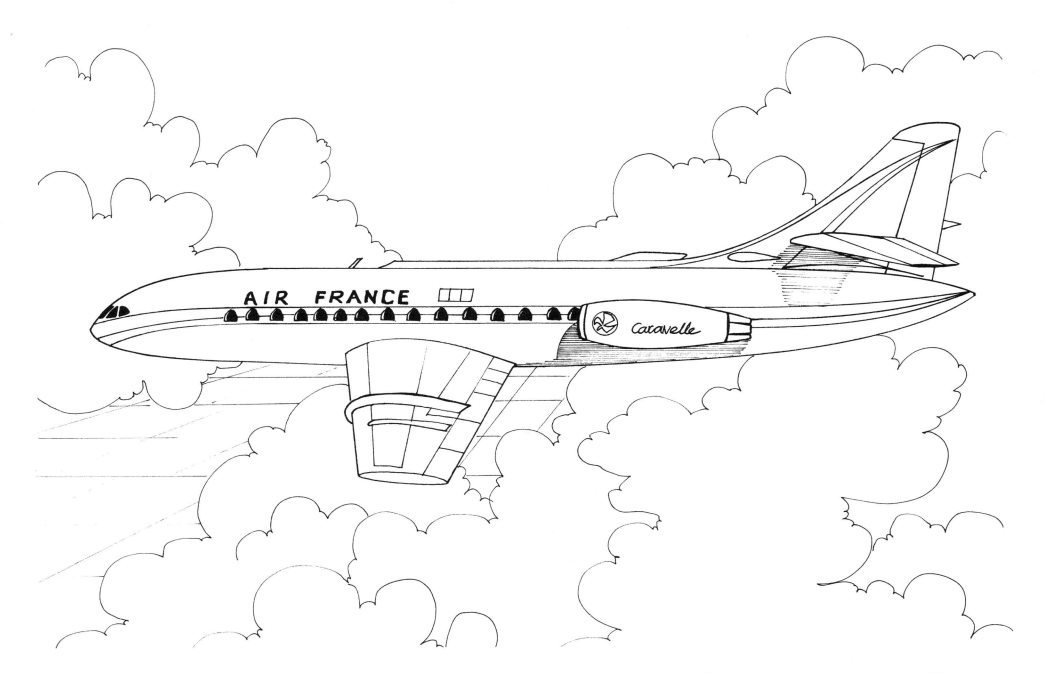

32. The Sud-Aviation Caravelle is an uncommon sight these days. The world's first short-haul jetliner, 282 Caravelles were built between the first prototype flight in 1955 and 1972.

33. The Vickers VC10 has the unusual configuration of four tail-mounted jet engines. First flown in 1962, it was designed to provide jet service in hot climates and at high altitudes, conditions seen at many airports in Africa.

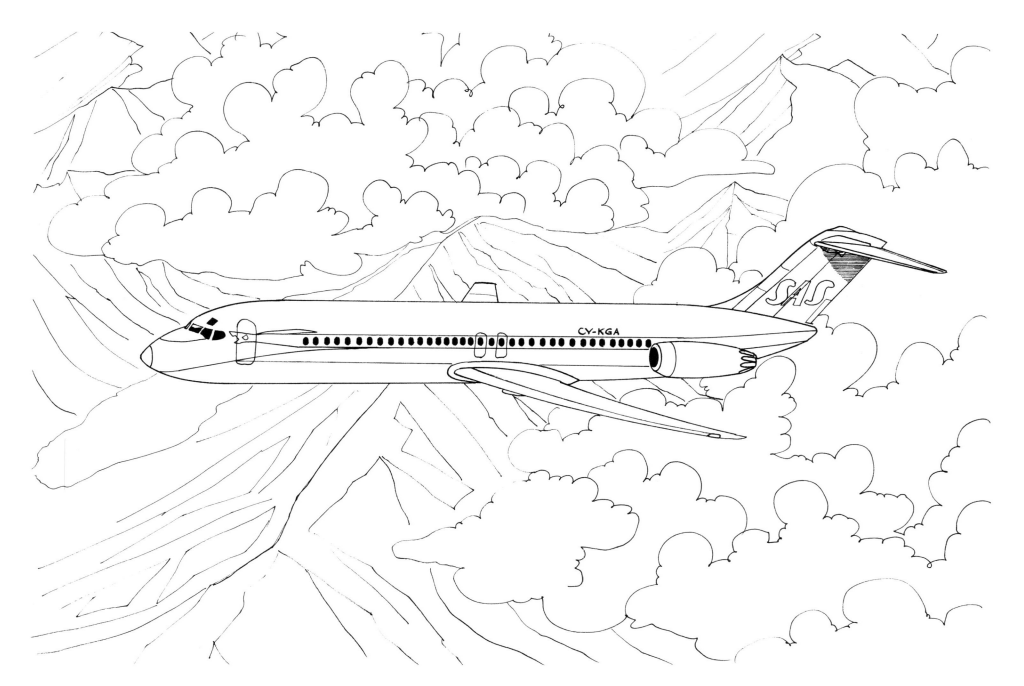

34. The Douglas DC-9 and its successor look-a-like McDonnell Douglas MD-80 series have been produced since 1965. Scandinavian Airlines System's fleet of 97 is based at hubs in the capitals of Denmark, Norway, and Sweden.

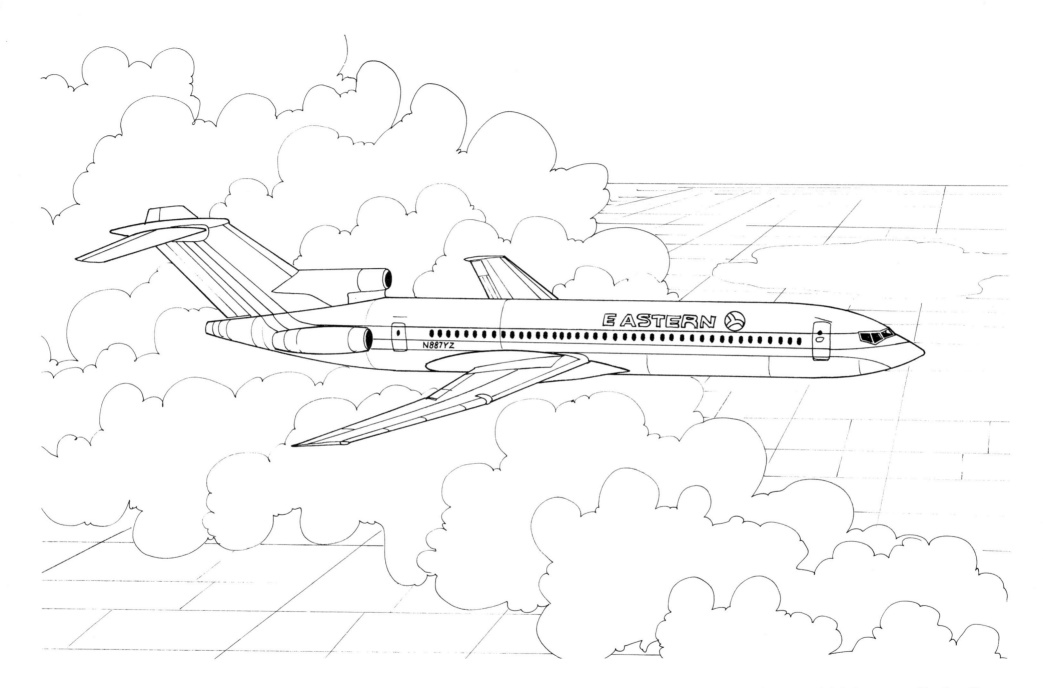

35. A workhorse in action worldwide, the Boeing 727 has been flying since 1963. Over 1800 have rolled off the assembly line, making it one of the most numerous jetliners ever built.

36. Lockheed's jumbo L-1011 TriStar can carry 400 passengers 2700 miles. Lockheed halted production in 1984 after 250 had been built.

37. Japan Air Lines operates 65 Boeing 747s. With a capacity of up 500 passengers, the 747 is the largest jetliner in operation.

Index

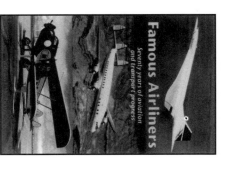